P9-DMK-290

A
GOOD
BOOK
FOR A
BAD
DAY

A GOOD BOOK FOR A BAD DAY

Erin McHugh

Andrews McMeel
PUBLISHING®

CONTENTS

INTRODUCTION

So out of the 365 days in a year, how many times do you say, "This is waaay too hard. Will this day ever be over?"

Wait, don't answer that—that number might just be too scary. But now, you can tuck this little book away to help you navigate through the low spots that seem to come along and ruin a perfectly good day. Unruly bosses. Ex-lovers. Bounced checks. Bird poop. All in a day's work, but now you can turn that beat around and check in with some folks who have some insight on how to chase away the ugly.

Everyone's here: from Sigmund Freud to Whoopi Goldberg, Coco Chanel to Lemony Snicket, John Waters to Jimi Hendrix. Everyone here has plenty to say to help you forget your woes and worries and to remind you how to live, love, and have some fun.

Because on a bad day, you need something with the perfect tidbits of verbal first aid to chase the blues away. Something like a combination sourcebook, talisman, 1,001-jokes book, and a playbook for life. Lucky for you, you happen to be holding it in your hand right now. So close your eyes, pick a page, and get ready to turn your crummy day around. This is a good book for a bad day.

LOVE

Love doesn't make the world
go round. Love is what makes
the ride worthwhile.

Franklin P. Jones

I wonder what fool it was
that first invented kissing.

Jonathan Swift

Love is a game that two
can play and both win.

Eva Gabor

Love loves to love love.

James Joyce

The secret of a happy
marriage remains a secret.

Henny Youngman

A kiss is a lovely trick designed
by nature to stop speech when
words become superfluous.

Ingrid Bergman

If it is your time, love will track
you down like a cruise missile.

Lynda Barry

When the power of love
overcomes the love of power,
the world will know peace.

Jimi Hendrix

One is very crazy when in love.

Sigmund Freud

Love is the magician that pulls
man out of his own hat.

Ben Hecht

I thank God I was raised Catholic,
so sex will always be dirty.

John Waters

The Eskimos had fifty-two
names for snow because it was
important to them; there ought
to be as many for love.

Margaret Atwood

In my sex fantasy, nobody
ever loves me for my mind.

Nora Ephron

I love you and it's getting worse.

Joseph E. Morris

A heart that loves is always young.

Greek proverb

Love does not consist in
gazing at each other, but in
looking outward together
in the same direction.

Antoine de Saint-Exupéry

And in the end, the love you take
is equal to the love you make.

Paul McCartney

Love is a serious mental disease.

Plato

There are never enough
"I love you's."

Lenny Bruce

I want
To do with you what spring does
   with the cherry trees.

Pablo Neruda

You know you're in love
when you can't fall asleep
because reality is finally better
than your dreams.

Dr. Seuss

We accept the love we
think we deserve.

Stephen Chbosky

Never love anyone who treats
you like you're ordinary.

Oscar Wilde

Love is a fire. But whether
it is going to warm your hearth
or burn down your house,
you can never tell.

Joan Crawford

I stay cool and dig all jive,
That's the way I stay alive.
My motto,
as I live and learn,
is
Dig and be dug
In return.

Langston Hughes

MONEY

The lack of money is the root of all evil.

Mark Twain

Before borrowing money from a friend,
decide which you need most.

Henry Fielding

Money is the best deodorant.

Elizabeth Taylor

I don't like money, actually,
but it quiets my nerves.

Joe Louis

Sex is like money;
only too much is enough.

John Updike

I'd like to live as a poor man
with lots of money.

Pablo Picasso

All I ask is the chance to prove that
money can't make me happy.

Spike Milligan

People say that money is not the key to happiness, but I always figured if you have enough money, you can have a key made.

Joan Rivers

Money is a terrible master
but an excellent servant.

P.T. Barnum

One of the secrets of a happy life
is continuous small treats.

Iris Murdoch

Take care of the luxuries
and the necessities will take
care of themselves.

Dorothy Parker

He who hesitates is poor.

Mel Brooks

I'm living so far beyond my
income that we may almost be
said to be living apart.

e. e. cummings

I made my money the
old-fashioned way. I was very
nice to a wealthy relative
right before he died.

Malcolm Forbes

SUCCESS

Courage is being scared to death
but saddling up anyway.

John Wayne

The question isn't who is going to
let me; it's who is going to stop me.

Ayn Rand

Ambition is a dream
with a V8 engine.

Elvis Presley

If your ship doesn't come in,
swim out to it!

Jonathan Winters

If my mind can conceive it,
if my heart can believe it,
I know I can achieve it.

Jesse Jackson

It is not enough to succeed.
Others must fail.

Gore Vidal

My formula for success is
rise early, work late, and strike oil.

J. Paul Getty

It is more fun to be the painter
than the paint.

George Clooney

The worst part of success
is trying to find someone who
is happy for you.

Bette Midler

We are all of us stars,
and we deserve to twinkle.

Marilyn Monroe

Same.

Someone's sitting in the shade
today because someone planted
a tree a long time ago.

Warren Buffett

I'd rather regret the things
I've done than the things
I haven't done.

Lucille Ball

Find something you're
passionate about and keep
tremendously interested in it.

Julia Child

Start where you are.
Use what you have.
Do what you can.

Arthur Ashe

You gotta stop wearing
your wishbone where your
backbone ought to be.

Clementine Paddleford

The distance between
insanity and genius is measured
only by success.

Ian Fleming

The minute you settle for less
than you deserve, you get even
less than you settled for.

Maureen Dowd

Only the mediocre are
always at their best.

Jean Giraudoux

Everybody has a plan
until they get hit.

Mike Tyson

You can, you should, and if you're brave enough to start, you will.

Stephen King

If you're going to be
thinking anything, you might
as well think big.

Donald Trump

A hero is no braver than an
ordinary man, but he is braver
five minutes longer.

Ralph Waldo Emerson

Confidence is 10 percent hard
work and 90 percent delusion.

Tina Fey

The biggest risk is not taking
any risk. . . . In a world that's
changing really quickly, the only
strategy that is guaranteed to
fail is not taking risks.

Mark Zuckerberg

The only thing that ever sat
its way to success was a hen.

Sarah Brown

FRIENDSHIP

Lots of people want to ride
with you in the limo, but what
you want is someone who will
take the bus with you when
the limo breaks down.

Oprah Winfrey

A real friend is one who
walks in when the rest of
the world walks out.

Walter Winchell

Whoever is happy will
make others happy too.

Anne Frank

The smile is the shortest
distance between two people.

Victor Borge

The friend who holds your
hand and says the wrong thing
is made of dearer stuff than
the one who stays away.

Barbara Kingsolver

What is a friend?
A single soul dwelling in two bodies.

Aristotle

My definition of a friend is somebody who adores you even though they know the things you're most ashamed of.

Jodie Foster

My friends are my "estate."

Emily Dickinson

The best time to make friends
is before you need them.

Ethel Barrymore

There is nothing better
than a friend, unless it is a
friend with chocolate.

Linda Grayson

Love is blind.
Friendship closes its eyes.

Friedrich Nietzsche

The capacity for friendship
is God's way of apologizing
for our families.

Jay McInerney

Only your real friends will tell
you when your face is dirty.

Sicilian proverb

FAMILY

If you cannot get rid of the
family skeleton, you may as
well make it dance.

George Bernard Shaw

Happiness is having a large,
loving, caring, close-knit family
in another city.

George Burns

Adults are always asking kids
what they want to be when
they grow up because they are
looking for ideas.

Paula Poundstone

In time of test, family is best.

Burmese proverb

One day you will do things for me that you hate. That is what it means to be family.

Jonathan Safran Foer

So live that you wouldn't be
ashamed to sell the family parrot
to the town gossip.

Will Rogers

Home is where you are loved
the most and act the worst.

Marjorie Pay Hinckley

Sticking with your family is
what *makes* it a family.

Mitch Albom

A dysfunctional family is
any family with more than
one person in it.

Mary Karr

Before most people start boasting
about their family tree, they
usually do a good pruning job.

O. A. Battista

The problem with the gene pool
is that there's no lifeguard.

David Gerrold

There is no such thing as fun
for the whole family.

Jerry Seinfeld

FUN

Wine is constant proof that God
loves us and loves to see us happy.

Benjamin Franklin

Why not just live in the moment,
especially if it has a good beat?

Goldie Hawn

One cannot have too large a party.

Jane Austen

Buy the ticket, take the ride.

Hunter S. Thompson

My motto is: more good times.

Jack Nicholson

Life is like hot jazz . . . it's best
when you improvise.

George Gershwin

If you're going to be able to
look back at something and laugh
about it, you might as well
laugh about it now.

Marie Osmond

Yield to temptation. It may
not pass your way again.

Robert Heinlein

There is no sunrise so
beautiful that it is worth
waking me up to see it.

Mindy Kaling

Wrinkles will only go where
the smiles have been.

Jimmy Buffett

What soap is to the body,
laughter is to the soul.

Yiddish proverb

Don't take your toys inside
just because it's raining.

Cher

Half working, half dancing—
that is the right mixture.

Elisabeth Kübler-Ross

You can't learn everything
you need to know legally.

John Irving

If we'd only stop trying
to be happy, we could have
a pretty good time.

Edith Wharton

Anything worth doing is
worth overdoing.

Mick Jagger

A good laugh and a long sleep are
the two best cures for anything.

Irish proverb

HOPE

When you reach the end of your rope, tie a knot in it and hang on.

Franklin D. Roosevelt

Hope is the physician
of each misery.

Irish proverb

Children are happy because they don't have a file in their minds called "All the Things That Could Go Wrong."

Marianne Williamson

If you love life,
life will love you back.

Arthur Rubinstein

Only when it is dark enough
can you see the stars.

Martin Luther King, Jr.

Don't give up.
Don't lose hope.
Don't sell out.

Christopher Reeve

Hope will never be silent.

Harvey Milk

We *all* hope.
It's what keeps us alive.

David Mamet

Don't let your dreams be dreams.

Jack Johnson

SELF

I got my own back.

Maya Angelou

If you smile when no one else is around, you really mean it.

Andy Rooney

A person who knows how
to laugh at himself will never
cease to be amused.

Shirley MacLaine

Normal is nothing more than a
cycle on a washing machine.

Whoopi Goldberg

Maybe your weird is my normal.
Who's to say?

Nicki Minaj

They can't scare me if
I scare them first.

Lady Gaga

It ain't what they call you,
it's what you answer to.

W. C. Fields

When you come out of the storm, you won't be the same person who walked in. That's what this storm's all about.

Haruki Murakami

Don't you dare underestimate
the power of your own instinct.

Barbara Corcoran

Always be a first-rate version of yourself, instead of a second-rate version of somebody else.

Judy Garland

I wasn't lucky. I deserved it.

Margaret Thatcher

I don't do drugs. I am drugs.

Salvador Dalí

Accept that some days you
are the pigeon, and some days
you are the statue.

Scott Adams

Don't compromise yourself.
You're all you've got.

Janis Joplin

Trust yourself. You know more
than you think you do.

Benjamin Spock

It's sad to grow old,
but nice to ripen.

Brigitte Bardot

Superman don't need no seat belt.

Muhammad Ali

I don't want everyone to
like me; I should think less of
myself if some people did.

Henry James

I am bigger than the box I'm in.

Rachel Cohn

People who do not value
you are worthless, and those
who do are priceless.

Amit Abraham

One of the keys to happiness
is a bad memory.

Rita Mae Brown

When you are happy, you can
forgive a great deal.

Princess Diana

Happiness is always an inside job.

Anonymous

There's only one thing
I never did and wish I had done:
climb a fence.

Queen Mary

As far as I'm concerned, I prefer silent vice to ostentatious virtue.

Albert Einstein

Joy is the best makeup.

Anne Lamott

I'd far rather be happy
than right any day.

Douglas Adams

LIFE

Don't wait. The time will
never be just right.

Napoleon Hill

I tell you, we are here on
earth to fart around, and don't
let anyone tell you different.

Kurt Vonnegut

The life you have led doesn't need
to be the only life you have.

Anna Quindlen

I am not influenced by other human beings. But I am inspired.

Elaine Stritch

One must never look for
happiness: one meets it by the way.

Isabelle Eberhardt

Anything can happen.
Anything happens all the time.

Jonathan Tropper

Life is what you make it.
Always has been, always will be.

Eleanor Roosevelt

I think everybody should get rich
and famous and do everything
they ever dreamed of so they can
see it's not the answer.

Jim Carrey

Stay hungry, stay foolish.

Steve Jobs

Don't let yesterday use up
too much of today.

Will Rogers

If you don't live it, it won't
come out of your horn.

Charlie Parker

Rebellion is the only thing
that keeps you alive!

Marianne Faithfull

Life is rather like a tin
of sardines—we're all of us
looking for the key.

Alan Bennett

Dream as if you'll live forever.
Live as if you'll die today.

James Dean

If we wait until we're ready, we'll
be waiting for the rest of our lives.

Lemony Snicket

I hope life isn't a big joke,
because I don't get it.

Jack Handey

I have a simple philosophy.
Fill what's empty.
Empty what's full.
And scratch where it itches.

Alice Roosevelt Longworth

The best things in life
are free. The second best
are very expensive.

Coco Chanel

I love living. I have some problems with my life, but living is the best thing they've come up with so far.

Neil Simon

Andrews McMeel Publishing
a division of Andrews McMeel Universal
1130 Walnut Street, Kansas City, Missouri 64106

www.andrewsmcmeel.com

Illustration by Anne Reynolds

17 18 19 20 21 SHO 10 9 8 7 6 5 4 3

ISBN: 978-1-4494-6217-8

Library of Congress Control Number: 2014941955

ATTENTION: SCHOOLS AND BUSINESSES

Andrews McMeel books are available at quantity discounts with bulk purchase for educational, business, or sales promotional use. For information, please e-mail the Andrews McMeel Publishing Special Sales Department: specialsales@amuniversal.com.

If you're interested in learning more
about our books, find us on Facebook at
Andrews McMeel Publishing and follow
us on Twitter: **@AndrewsMcMeel**.

www.andrewsmcmeel.com